T0194902

A Prince and His Father

CAROLE DEFFES KELLY

WestBow Press books may be ordered through booksellers or by contacting:

WestBow Press
A Division of Thomas Nelson & Zondervan
1663 Liberty Drive
Bloomington, IN 47403
www.westbowpress.com
1 (866) 928-1240

ISBN: 978-1-9736-3728-8 (sc)
ISBN: 978-1-9736-3729-5 (e)

Library of Congress Control Number: 2018909886

Print information available on the last page.

WestBow Press rev. date: 08/21/2018

WESTBOW
PRESS®
A DIVISION OF THOMAS NELSON
& ZONDERVAN

Part

1

"The True Story of Christmas"

God created our world, and it was perfect.

Then God created the first man and woman.

He made them a beautiful garden in which to live.

They could eat from all trees in the garden except one.

God told them not to eat from the Tree of Knowledge, of good and evil, or they would die.

The devil, Satan, is evil. He disguised himself as a beautiful snake. He told Eve she would not die if she ate from the forbidden tree, but she would be wise like God.

So, Eve ate from the tree and gave some to Adam. They both disobeyed God. Because they listened to Satan, he became their master.

That's how sin started in our world.

Then Adam and Eve had children, and their children were born into sin. Every child after that was born into sin; even today, thousands of year later.

God the Father and his Son, the Prince, are sinless and live in heaven. They agreed that our world needs a Savior. The Prince loves all people in the world, and he wanted to be our Savior, but he had to be born as a baby.

Now there was a young girl named Mary. She was getting ready to marry Joseph. God sent an angel to Mary and told her that God chose her to be the mother of his son, the Prince. Mary was pleased that God chose her.

God put the Prince as a seed in Mary's body to grow as a baby and be born as we are.

God sent an angel to Joseph and told him not to be afraid to marry Mary, because she was carrying God's child in her body.

Joseph took Mary out of town because people wouldn't understand.

He walked, and Mary rode on a donkey.

The Bible foretold many years before that a King would be born in Bethlehem. There were astrologers and astronomers who were wise men. The wise men got on their camels and followed a bright star that God put in the sky. They found the Prince and brought him gifts of Gold, Frankincense, and Myrrh.

Nearby were shepherds watching their sheep.

An angel appeared to them and told them the good news. A Savior was born in Bethlehem.

The shepherds went to see the Prince.

The sky was filed with angels praising God.

We celebrate Christmas because a Prince was born to save us all from sin and evil. That Prince is Jesus, God's only son.

Jesus is God the Father's gift to us.

That is the true story of Christmas.

The Christmas Tree represents God's creation, life, happiness, and his love for all of us.

Our gifts to others represent God's gift to us, his only son, Jesus Christ.

Part

2

"The True Story of Easter"

While Jesus was still a baby in Bethlehem, an angel came to Joseph in a dream and said, "Get Up"! Flee to Egypt with Mary and Jesus where they will be safe. For King Herod, a wicked King, was so angry when he heard a King was born. He ordered babies under the age of 2 to be killed, because he wanted to be the only King.

Not long after, King Herod died. God told Joseph to bring Mary and Jesus back to the land of Israel. So, they settled in the town of Nazareth, where Jesus continued to grow in grace and wisdom.

Many years before Jesus came, when a person sinned, they would kill and sacrifice an animal.

The animal took the place of the person because God said that sin had to die.

Now when we sin, Jesus has covered our sin. He sacrificed himself one time for all people.

Jesus is now around the age of 30.

There was a preacher named John the Baptizer.

John loved God and baptized people in the Jordan River.

Jesus went to John to be baptized. When Jesus came out of the water; the spirit of God, in the form of a dove, came to Jesus. From heaven, God said, "This is my beloved son in whom I am well pleased."

This is when Jesus' ministry started.

Thousands of people followed Jesus. He had compassion and loved everyone. He healed the sick, the blind, and the crippled. He fed thousands of people and raised some from the dead. Jesus was God in a human body, just as they planned in heaven.

Jesus began to gather and teach his disciples.

They would carry on his work after Jesus went back to heaven.

There were religious groups of men called the Pharisees, Sadducees and the Scribes. They looked holy, but only on the outside. They memorized the Bible, but it wasn't in their hearts. They acted religious to get praise and money from the people.

They saw Jesus ride in on a donkey, and all the people threw out palm branches and were praising him.

The Religious leaders hated him. They were afraid that they would lose all their power and money because the people were following Jesus and not them.

The night before Jesus died, he had the Last Supper with his 12 disciples.

Jesus told them the plan that He and His Father made in heaven. Jesus would die for all sins.

The religious leaders got the temple guards to get Jesus in the middle of the night while he was praying in the Garden of Gethsemane. They brought Jesus to the high priest, then to Pontius Pilate, the governor of Rome. Jesus was beaten. They wanted him gone.

Envy and jealousy are terrible things.

The governor, Pontius Pilate, gave Jesus over to his accusers to be crucified.

Jesus carried his cross, with help, to Golgotha, where he died for you and me. All our sins were nailed to that cross just like God the Father and Jesus planned in heaven.

Jesus was buried in a tomb, which was a cave.

The Roman guards rolled a large stone in front of it and sealed it.

On the 3rd day, at sunrise, Mary Magdalen and a few women went to Jesus' tomb. The tomb was open, and the stone was rolled away. Mary looked in and saw an angel. The angel said to the women, "Jesus is not here, he has risen. Go quickly and tell his disciples."

Jesus' disciples were in the Upper Room and Jesus appeared to them. He wanted them to see he died and came to life again, as he said he would.

Jesus appeared to more than 500 people. His mission in our world was completed. He went back to his home in heaven.

His disciples carried on the good news. Jesus came down from heaven to save us from our sin and God's wrath and judgement.

Heaven is Jesus' home and it's our home, too.

Jesus

From Heaven
To
The
Manger

From the manger – to the cross – back to heaven

Revelation 1:17 & 18

Do not be afraid;
I am the First and
the last.
I am alive forever more.

Put your trust in Jesus and his death on the cross, than God's Holy Spirit will come live in your heart forever. He will guide you through your life.

Believe in Jesus. Draw close to him, and he will draw close to you.

That's the true story of Easter.

John 1:14

The word (Jesus) became flesh and dwelt among us.

Printed in the United States
By Bookmasters